*Will our children l*

# BRiNGiNG UP
# RESPONSiBLE
# CHiLDREN

John Sharry

*VERITAS*

First published 1999 by
Veritas Publications
7/8 Lower Abbey Street
Dublin 1

Copyright © John Sharry 1999

ISBN 1 85390 414 7

Design: Bill Bolger
Cover illustration: Angela Hampton Family Life Pictures
© Angela Hampton
Cartoons: John Byrne
Printed in the Republic of Ireland by Betaprint Ltd, Dublin

# CONTENTS

*I wish to acknowledge the contribution of my colleague, Professor Carol Fitzpatrick, co-author of the Parents Plus Programme, in the development of these ideas*

# INTRODUCTION

## LOVING AND RESPONSIBLE PARENTING

With increased pressures on families, being a parent these days can be a difficult task. With less support from extended family and the community, families sometimes feel more isolated than they did in the past. Parents, especially mothers, often have to balance expectations both to have successful careers and to be excellent parents at home. In addition there is the scrutiny from outside: there is much debate as to what is good parenting, and bigger expectations for parents to achieve this. We are much more aware of the need of children to receive unconditional love and affirmation and how this is vital for them to grow up into happy, confident and independent adults. Yet we are also aware of the dangers of over-liberal parenting, and none of us wants our children to be spoiled or out of control.

I DON'T KNOW ABOUT YOU, BUT AS A PARENT I'M STARTING TO FEEL ISOLATED...

Many parents are confused as to what is the best way to discipline children. Many of the authoritarian means of discipline (such as physical punishment) which we were brought up with are being increasingly questioned. Yet there is little information on effective alternatives. Often being responsible and being loving as a parent seem to be in contradiction. How can parents maintain a good and loving relationship with their children while also teaching what is right and wrong and helping them learn good social behaviour? This booklet attempts to provide an answer to this question, by setting out a step-by-step guide for parents who want to positively encourage their children to behave well and to achieve their full potential, while also maintaining a satisfying and enjoyable relationship with them. The focus is on the young child (aged two to ten years), when parents can have a great influence and hopefully set the stage for a more peaceful adolescence!

Before we go through the nine steps, let's first look at the reasons for misbehaviour in young children.

## Misbehaviour is Normal

All children, from time to time, show problem behaviour such as tantrums, defiance, lying and even stealing. Although stressful for parents, these problems are common in childhood. Research shows that, on average, children comply with between a third and two thirds of their parents' requests of them. This means that defiance is pretty normal. It is important not to see defiance as a personalised attack on your authority but rather as your child's normal testing of your rules and limits. Children form their identities by clashing with their parents' values and rules. It is part of their development of independence and their discovery of themselves as separate people.

## Why Behavioural Problems?

When people see a child who is 'bold' or out of control, there is often much debate as to who is at fault. People often blame the parents, thinking they are not managing the child 'right', or, alternatively, they blame the child, thinking there is something inherently wrong with him or her.

There are many different reasons as to why children get into patterns of misbehaving; sometimes it is due to the child's particular temperament or the fact that they have special needs; sometimes it is due to the parents' own difficulties (stress, marital problems, depression) which are causing them to respond in inconsistent ways; often it is simply a normal phase of development where the child is testing limits. Whatever the cause, a blaming approach is always unhelpful and only adds to the problems. This booklet is less interested in finding a cause and more interested in helping parents to find solutions and to create more satisfying ways of relating to their children. The focus is on the interaction between parent and child – when parents respond differently to their children, they help their children behave differently. The goal is to help parents find new ways of responding to their children which are more positive and which in turn help children to change positively.

### Each Family is Different

Ask any parent who has more than one child whether each one was different to bring up and they will invariably say yes. One child may be very active and demanding while another may be placid and reserved. Children respond differently to traumatic family events, such as separation or illness. Some get angry and take their feelings out on everyone, some become very withdrawn, while some cope very well and are little affected. Each child has different needs and requires a different approach. Demanding children or children with special difficulties often need extra support and attention and require parents to respond extra consistently.

Equally, each parent's situation is different. We all have different temperaments, different values and different life experiences. We will all respond differently to our children and there is no one way to be as a parent. For these reasons, there is no expert prescription for what will work best with your child or in your family. While there are good guidelines and advice, you are the expert about your own children. Find out what works for you and your family. Trust your intuition.

## NINE STEPS TO BETTER BEHAVIOUR

In the following pages we will look at nine principles which, if applied over time, can make a real difference in improving your children's behaviour and helping you achieve a closer and more satisfying relationship with them. The nine principles are derived from a ten-week parenting course (the Parents Plus Programme) which is offered in many clinics throughout Ireland. The nine principles can be viewed as steps which can be followed, one-by-one, over the next few weeks. Most of these techniques will be familiar to you and recognisable as the good habits of parenting to which we all aspire. While these techniques are well proven as helpful to most families, none apply in every situation and in every context. It is important to adapt the ideas to your own unique family situation.

You will notice that the first few steps look at positive ways to encourage good behaviour in children, followed by the steps designed to help you with handling misbehaviour. I suggest that you start at the beginning, as the techniques on handling misbehaviour only work when you have already built a close, positive relationship with your children.

# STEP 1

## PARENTS CARING FOR THEMSELVES

Many parents with good intentions become martyrs to their children. In a desire to be truly loving and present with their children they give up everything of their own. They may give up work, or stop pursuing their interests or going out socially, or they may simply stop prioritising time for their own relaxation. Over time this can lead to resentment, and the parents' unacknowledged anger at the 'loss' of their own life builds up, or it can lead to parents being run down with little energy to pursue anything. From both these positions, it is hard to relate in a consistent, loving way to your children.

It is crucial for parents to look after their own needs as well as those of their children. When parents' own needs for care, comfort and fulfilment are met they are freed up to attend fully to the parenting role. Children need cared-for parents as much as they need parents to care for them. Love begins with self-love. We cannot love another unless we love and value ourselves. The best way to help our children to be confident people with high self-esteem is for us as parents to model this – to take steps to value, love and prioritise ourselves.

### HOW PARENTS CAN CARE FOR THEMSELVES

You may protest that in your busy life you simply can't afford to take time out for yourself. The reality is that you can't afford not to. Think about the times when you have been run down or feeling low and how it was impossible to do any of the more important tasks. Remember the times you felt energetic and good about yourself and how easy it was then to achieve things, and to be kind and loving to others. A little a bit of self-care goes a long way.

I recognise that building a routine of self-care can be very difficult for many parents who have a long history of 'serving others' to the exclusion of themselves, or who have a long history of putting themselves down or viewing themselves in a negative light. Nevertheless, to paraphrase the ancient Chinese proverb, even the longest journey starts with a single step. This first step could be going out of your way to get a babysitter, or insisting that your children go to bed on time to give you some space. Below is a list of ways parents have described on courses as beginning steps to self-caring:

- Going for a daily walk
- Spending time alone
- Getting up early to exercise
- Doing self-nurturing things like having a special bath
- Allowing their partners to cook a romantic meal once a week

## BUILD ON YOUR STRENGTHS AS A PARENT

You will notice that, throughout this booklet, I encourage you to build on your children's strengths and abilities. I also encourage you to apply the same principles to yourself. Too often parents give themselves a hard time, criticising their own behaviour and putting themselves down. Too often they focus on what they do wrong in every situation, thinking 'I wish I hadn't lost my patience like that', or 'I should have more time for my children'. Similarly, parents in couple relationships can relate negatively to each other, focusing on what the other has done wrong: 'I don't like the way you interrupted me talking to the kids' or 'You shouldn't have lost your temper then'.

I encourage you to break this negative pattern and reverse it. Start looking for what you and your partner are doing *right* as parents. Be on the lookout for the small steps of improvement you make each day, the times you manage successfully. Begin to notice what you like about yourself as a parent. Don't be afraid to praise yourself: 'I'm pleased at how I was firm in that instance' or 'I'm glad that at least I tried my best'. Equally, be on the lookout for examples of behaviour you like in your partner: 'Thanks for supporting me with Joe like that' or 'I'm really pleased that you came home early and we have some time to ourselves'.

It is in your children's interests for you to identify your own strengths and successes. Children learn a powerful lesson from you when you model self-encouragement. They learn how to be confident and successful and how to relate positively to other people.

Often parents go through difficult periods when it is hard for them to be consistent or to give their children all the time they deserve. At times like these, the worst thing parents can do is excessively blame themselves or be over-defensive. It is better to try to learn from the experience, acknowledge what needs to be done differently and move on. Self-compassion is as important as compassion toward others. It is powerful modelling for children to see their parents being honest about their mistakes and not dwelling on them but moving on to make a fresh start. This helps children learn how to move on from misbehaviour in the same way.

Remember, the goal is not to be a perfect parent or to have a perfect child. Such people do not exist (and if they did they would be unbearable to be around!). Rather, the goal is to be a 'good enough' parent – someone who accepts themselves as good enough, appreciates their own strengths as well as their weaknesses, tries their best and learns from experience.

TIPS FOR GOING FORWARD

1) Set aside a special time for yourself in the next week, doing something you really enjoy.

2) Promise to think positively about yourself over the next week. Look for examples of your good parenting.

DAD, IT'S TIME WE TALKED ABOUT THE FACTS OF LIFE... SUCH AS THE FACT THAT YOU'VE GOT TO LOOK AFTER YOURSELF...

# STEP 2

## PROVIDING POSITIVE ATTENTION TO CHILDREN

Have you noticed how young children will do anything to get their parents' attention? Having their parents notice and respond to them is probably the greatest reward for children and they will seek this in as many ways as possible. Often parents find ways of giving approving, loving attention to their children, with warm hugs, close conversations and kind words. These are good habits and are very healthy for parent and child. Unfortunately, parents often unwittingly provide attention negatively via shouting, criticising and even slapping. Strange as it may seem, these negative interactions are preferable to no attention at all and children will seek them out in place of being ignored.

We know from research that when attention is given to a certain behaviour, that behaviour tends to be repeated and to develop, while behaviour that is not given attention disappears. It is human nature to get trapped into giving children more attention when they are misbehaving than when they are behaving well. For example, when two children are playing quietly together they are usually ignored until one of them starts an argument or begins whining. Parents respond rapidly to the child's negative behaviour,

MUM HOW COME YOU NEVER TALK TO ME?

ASK YOUR FATHER

often with criticism or scolding, thus providing attention for negative behaviour while ignoring the positive behaviour shown when the children were playing quietly. If this pattern is repeated often enough, it does not take long for children to learn from experience that fighting and whining get a lot of adult attention.

This can become a vicious cycle. A child who misbehaves gains attention from a parent in the form of shouting or criticising. This can leave both parent and child upset and angry. From this position the child is more likely to seek attention again with misbehaviour and the parent more likely to respond angrily and so the cycle repeats itself.

### CATCH YOUR CHILD BEING GOOD

So how can you break this cycle? Or even better, how can you turn it on its head so that it becomes a positive cycle? The best way to do this is to go out of your way to make sure your children get lots of positive attention and encouragement whenever they behave well – literally catch your child being good. This positive attention leaves both you and your child feeling more content and close to one another. From this position the child is more likely to seek attention positively by behaving well again and the parent is more likely to respond positively. Thus this new positive cycle is established.

It can be difficult to make this switch to positive attention, especially when you are not used to it, or if you have experienced a lot of difficult behaviour in the past. However, it can make a real difference if you give it a try, and let go of any resentment from past misbehaviour. One parent of a ten-year-old boy who attended a parenting course gave a good example of how she managed to do this. She had been involved in a lot of conflict over many years with her son. This usually started with him

refusing to get out of bed in the morning, while she repeatedly called him with increasing irritation, ending in a screaming match, which set the scene for the rest of the day. At the start of the course almost every interaction between this mother and her son involved conflict and hostility, and she couldn't imagine being able to find anything good about his behaviour to which she could pay positive attention.

However, when she stood back a bit from the situation and observed her son, she quickly saw that there were many previously unnoticed aspects of his behaviour which she could acknowledge with positive attention. When he brought his cup over to the sink after breakfast she smiled and thanked him. When he let his younger brother play a computer game with him she said 'it's very nice the way you are kind to your brother'. There were many other positive situations she was able to see and comment on. Her son's behaviour changed quite dramatically over a number of months and the relationship between them improved markedly.

## How to Give Positive Attention

Going out of our way to give positive attention can feel a little uncomfortable at first - in our culture we are not used to it. But it gets easier and feels more natural as you persist with it and find your own individual style. There is no one right way to provide positive attention. What is most important is that it is personal and experienced as genuine by both parent and child. With young children, a simple pat on the head or a warm smile can be enough. For older children you may want to specifically comment on the behaviour you like. For example, you could say 'I see you've started your homework, that's good' or 'I'm really pleased to see that you've come in on time'.

If you are used to a lot of difficult behaviour from your child and feel there is little you can notice that is positive, a good way to get started is to spend some time thinking about the things you like about your child. You might want to recall the times he or she behaved well in the past (however long ago!) or times you enjoyed together and felt close. When you have pictured some of these things in your mind, write down one or two of them. When you've made a list, keep it in a safe place and over the next few days, look for further things your child does that you like and begin to note these down also. As you collect more and more examples of good behaviour, your attitude toward your child will change. Then, when you're ready, you can share some of your observations with your child. By now you are giving some really good positive attention to him or her.

## Positive Attention can Divert Misbehaviour

Psychologists have found that much of children's misbehaviour is rewarded by the attention it receives. They have also found that a bout of misbehaviour often happens just after a period of good behaviour which has gone unnoticed. By attending to the good behaviour first you can give children the attention they are looking for and divert them from seeking the attention negatively. A good example of this comes from a time I was working with a mother and her seven-year-old son and four-year-old daughter. The mother was describing how her son was often aggressive toward his little sister and this concerned her greatly. As she was speaking I could observe the children out of the corner of my eye and I saw how the girl was beginning to annoy her brother. She was trying to take the figures he was playing with and he was beginning to get upset, taking them back from her. It struck me that he was on the point of hitting out, so, rather than let this escalate, I went over to him and said 'It can be hard playing with your little sister, but you're doing a good job, letting her have some of

I APPRECIATE YOUR PAYING ME POSITIVE ATTENTION, MUM... BUT IT MAKES IT A BIT DIFFICULT TO WIN AT 'HIDE AND SEEK'...

your toys'. He enjoyed the compliment, relaxed and then said 'look Zoe, you can play with these figures and I'll play with these ones'. In this way, a bout of misbehaviour was avoided, and the child was reinforced for sharing with his sister. Of course this tactic does not work every time, but it can be very powerful in diverting misbehaviour to notice the good (or slightly good) behaviour that precedes it.

## Can Children Be Given Too Much Attention?

Children can certainly be given too much negative attention for troublesome behaviour. Children who are constantly pestering their parents – pulling out of them and whining – have learned that this way of behaving is guaranteed to get a response. Instead, providing attention to children when they are not behaving in this way, for example, when they are quiet, pleasant and doing what is asked of them, will, over time, bring about positive changes in their behaviour.

Some parents may be reluctant to praise ordinary behaviour or give a lot of positive attention, fearing it will make their children big-headed or that they might become dependent on the praise they receive. Research shows that children who receive much praise and encouragement – especially for ordinary and simple things – turn out to be the most successful, confident and securely independent adults. When positive attention is genuine and sincere, it is very difficult, perhaps impossible, to provide too much.

## Focus on what you want

Catching children being good is essentially about switching your focus to attending to what you want rather than what you don't want. Often parents are very clear about the behaviour they don't want in their children – fighting, whingeing, staying out late, etc. – but are less clear about what they *do* want from them. Instead of your two older children squabbling and fighting all day, what behaviour would you like to see? Perhaps you would like to see them getting along better, or sharing, or playing quietly together. Catching children being good is about thinking in advance about what you want and going out of your way to notice this behaviour and make a big deal when it occurs.

Remember also to catch yourself being good as a parent. As I have said earlier it is important to apply these positive principles to yourself as well as to your children.

Making a shift to consistently focus on what you *want*, rather than what you don't want, can make a real difference in your life, transforming your own sense of self, your relationship with your children and with your partner.

TIPS FOR GOING FORWARD
1) Make a note of the specific times your children behave well or better than usual. Be on the lookout to catch them being good.
2) Notice things that happen in your family that you are pleased about and that you would like to see happen again.
3) Sit down and make a list of your goals as a parent. Write down what you would like for your children and also for yourself as a parent.

# STEP 3

## Play and Special Time with Children

In Step 2 we talked about the importance of parents positively attending to their children, particularly by catching them being good. Now we look at how parents can further promote a positive interaction with their children by setting aside special time to play with them.

Often parents will do everything for their children, except play with them. They will feed and dress them, take them to and from school and ensure they get to bed on time, but in their busy schedule there can be little time left to sit down and play or spend relaxed, fun time with them. Often busy weeks can pass with little quality time spent between parent and child.

There is an idea in society that play between parents and their children is an unimportant activity and a low priority, given all the other things that need to be done. Yet the truth is very far from this. Good play is essential to the well-being and development of children, and play between parent and child is not only rewarding and enjoyable in itself, it also builds a close parent-child relationship which forms the basis for solving discipline problems.

### The Value of Play and Special Time for Children

Play promotes physical, educational, emotional and social development in young children. Through play (aside from having fun), they learn new skills and abilities, express feelings and learn how to get along with other children. It is extremely important for parents to take special time to play with their children for many reasons:

- Playtime can be a relaxing and enjoyable experience for parents as well as for children. In fact, many parents describe these times as among their happiest. Good playtime is a reward in itself to parents, providing an often missed opportunity to enjoy their child's company away from stress and conflict.

- Playtime brings parent and child closer. Children are more likely to open up to parents before and after playtime. With older children it is often during shared activities that they will reveal concerns or special interests they have. Parents can really get to know their children by spending special time with them.

- Child-centred play allows children to take the lead and make decisions. Children who experience their parents giving them control in play situations are more likely to have a sufficient sense of security to allow their parents to take control in discipline situations. When parents respect children's rules in play, children are more likely in turn to respect parents' rules in other situations.

## How Best to Play with Children

While there is no one right way to play with children, there are a number of guidelines, which can be helpful:

### Set aside a special time

Perhaps the most important thing to do is to set aside a special time to play with your children. In a busy parent's schedule, this may need to be planned in advance and prioritised as something important and not to be missed. Play sessions don't have to be long to be effective. With young children (up to six years of age) short daily play sessions of fifteen minutes can make a real difference. With slightly older children, you might want to have longer times less frequently (two one-hour sessions weekly) based around an activity or hobby.

### Spend one-on-one time with children

Special time works best if it only involves one child at a time. While this can put extra demands on parents with many children, there is no replacement for one-on-one time with another person, in terms of getting to know them deeply and building an enduring bond with them. Even it means slightly shorter or less frequent special times, it is still best to have quality one-on-one times with your children. These are the foundations of good family life.

I'VE ENJOYED OUR "ONE-ON-ONE" TIME, TOO — NOW PLEASE GET OFF ME!

### Follow the child's lead

In good playtime, children should be encouraged to take charge and make most of the decisions. Children have many other arenas in life where parents are in charge, so playtime is their chance to try out decision-making and to develop confidence. Parents can sit back and follow the child's lead, valuing and affirming their imagination and initiative. With young children this simply means letting the child choose the game or activity and how to play it. With older children it means involving them in the planning of activities and future special time.

## Choose interactive, imaginative activities

The best toys and play materials are those which stimulate a child's imagination and creativity. They don't have to be expensive 'educational' toys. We all see children who turn away from the expensive toy to transform the box and wrapper into an imaginative castle!

The best type of toys allow children to be active and creative rather than passive (as with television viewing) and which allow parent and child to do things together. It is important to have toys which match a child's age and ability level as well as their personality. For older children, choose activities which emphasise co-operation and which allow you to interact with them. For example, going fishing is often a better choice than the cinema as it gives you more of an opportunity to talk and relate together. Below are some suggestions for play and special time to which you can add your own ideas:

### Younger children

- play dough, plasticine
- blocks / Lego (any building or construction kits)
- jigsaws (age level)
- dolls / figures / puppets
- tea set, tool set
- farmhouse, doll's house
- soft toys
- dress up box
- paints, crayons, colours

VERY CREATIVE, LOUISE...
MAYBE NEXT TIME
YOU COULD TRY USING
A LITTLE LESS
PLAY DOUGH?

*Older children*
- jigsaws
- construction kits/models (boats, planes, etc.)
- paints/colours
- creative activities such as making a collage
- board games
- football/outdoor games/special activities (fishing)

ENCOURAGE CHILDREN IN PLAY
It's easy to fall into the trap of correcting children when they play. Out of a desire to teach children, parents can find themselves being critical, saying 'Oh, that doesn't go there' or 'It should be done like this'. I suggest that for special playtime, you go out of your way to encourage children, looking for things they are doing right and showing great interest in their activities. For example, you can use lots of positive comments such as 'I like that colour you have chosen' or 'It was a good idea to turn it around that way' or 'You're really persistent trying to get this house made'. Essentially it is about being a good audience to children in their play, taking a great interest in what they are doing, getting down to their level, providing lots of eye contact and good body language. Using encouraging statements and kind comments helps children continue in their play and promotes a rewarding experience for both parent and child.

HAVE FAMILY SPECIAL TIME
As well as individual special time between parent and child, special time for the whole family together is important. Like playtime, this can get lost in the busy weekly schedule and often needs to be prioritised and planned in advance. Families can set aside a special Sunday meal, or family trip at the weekends as a way of spending relaxed, fun time together.

1) Set aside a regular special time to play or spend special time with your children individually. For young children, this could be short daily sessions of fifteen to twenty minutes. For older children, this could be less frequently but for a longer period of time, for example in the form of a weekly planned activity.

2) During special time make sure to follow the child's lead, use lots of encouragement and above all have fun.

# STEP 4

## Specific Encouragement And Praise
### 'Mol An Óige Agus Tiocfaidh Sí'

A parent told me about the above old Irish saying which means 'encourage the young and they will flourish'. I was heartened to hear it as quite often the Irish upbringing is one of discouragement. The Irish are sometimes the first to put each other down, to use sarcasm and to be negative and begrudging. However, the saying made me think that perhaps this negative thinking was only a recent phenomenon coming from a recent history of oppression, and that perhaps the deeper and older Irish spirit was one of positive encouragement. It is this attitude and way of life that Step 4 promotes.

### Specific Encouragement And Praise

People often think that the best way to change a child's misbehaviour is to criticise and scold them when they misbehave – pointing out the error of their ways, so to speak. However, this approach has a number of drawbacks: excessive criticism can damage a child's confidence and ability to change; it leaves both parent and child upset; and it gives attention to the misbehaviour. It is far more effective for the parent to encourage and praise the examples of good behaviour they see. By making this switch in focus you will notice an improvement in your relationship, as it is far more enjoyable and satisfying to encourage rather than criticise.

Often people think that children who are consistently 'bold' or 'naughty' need a lot criticism and don't deserve praise. The truth of the matter is that these children's confidence is such that they need encouragement far more than other children who are receiving it already. Helping these children see that there are some things that they can do right is the best way to help them get back on the road to improved behaviour and better relationships.

## SKILLS OF SPECIFIC ENCOURAGEMENT

When we use encouragement or praise to promote good behaviour in children, we can make sure it gets through to the child by ensuring that it is clear, specific and personal.

### *Encouragement should be clear*

You should have the child's full attention before you give encouraging statements. It is less effective to encourage with statements muttered under your breath from another part of the room or when the child is doing something else like watching TV and not really listening. It is important to get down to the child's level, to make eye contact and to use a warm and genuine tone of voice. The child should be in no doubt that he or she is getting a positive message from you. Think of encouragement as the most important message you can possibly give to your children. You really want to make sure it gets through to them.

### Encouragement should be specific

If you want to help children to change positively they need to know exactly which behaviour they are being praised for, and which qualities you are encouraging in them. Vague statements such as 'You are a great boy' or 'Good girl' don't tell a child what you are pleased about, and can soon wear thin and seem insincere. It is more effective to say, 'Thanks for putting out the bins when I asked' or 'It is great to see you sharing with your sister'. These statements help children know exactly what good behaviour you are praising and make it more likely to occur again. It is also important to praise as soon after the desired behaviour as possible so they are in no doubt that it is that behaviour you want to see again.

### Encouragement should be personal

The best way to encourage is unique to each parent and child. What is essential though, is that your child experiences your encouragement as personal and genuine. Saying how you feel and expressing this to your child can make a real difference. Often this can be achieved by using an 'I' message. For example:

'I really appreciate the way you cleaned up your room'; or
'Thanks for coming in immediately when I asked you, that means a lot to me'; or
'I really enjoyed playing with you today, I love it when we get on so well.'

It is also very important to be affectionate when encouraging children, especially when they are younger. A simple hug or a pat on the back can speak volumes. Remember, what works in encouragement varies from parent to parent and from child to child. Find out what works for you.

Often parents say that they never witness examples of the good behaviour they want in their children. For example, the children never do what they're asked, or they never share with other children. When you are feeling negative and angry it can be hard to notice the positives. However, if you closely observe your children you will notice that there are always times, however short-lived, when they are behaving more positively. If you are serious about helping your children change, it can make a real difference to notice these exceptions. Children need to know there are some things they are doing right, before they can have the confidence to change.

It is important not to wait for perfection or a finished task before you encourage or praise. Change can be gradual and, to ensure that children don't get demotivated, it is important to encourage and praise steps in the right direction. For example, encourage a child when she starts to do her homework, 'I'm pleased to see you sitting down straight away and starting your

homework'. You don't have to wait for the homework to be completed. Encouraging the first step of a task helps a child persist and continue to the end.

### DOUBLE ENCOURAGEMENT

The effect of encouragement can be doubled by involving other people. Praising a child in public or in front of important people can make it more powerful and really drive the message home. For example, if Dad has witnessed good behaviour, as well as praising it himself he can double the impact by telling Mum about it in front of the child later in the day. There is often a tendency to nag about misbehaviour, to really go on about what is wrong. Using encouragement, you can turn this around and really go on about what your child has done right.

### PERSIST WITH ENCOURAGEMENT

Many children initially reject encouragement and praise. They might shrug it off, saying, 'Of course I didn't do it right' or they may not believe the parent is genuine. If a child has not received much encouragement in the past, it can take a while before he or she can begin to accept the positives you point out. Equally, if encouragement is a new approach for parent and child it can feel awkward at first and, like any skill, it can take a while before it becomes second nature. It is important not to give up if a child initially rejects encouragement. See this as a sign

I'M SO PLEASED THAT YOU'VE STOPPED TELLING ALL THOSE LIES..

I DON'T BELIEVE YOU.

that your child needs the encouragement all the more. Persistence can really pay off.

Think about new ways to get your encouragement through. It might be a case of picking a better time or choosing different things to praise. It might help to change your style of encouragement to ensure it is clear, specific and personal. This all helps the child experience it as genuine. With older children it can be effective to sit down and talk about what it is you are pleased about and what it is you want from them. You can even explain your new positive approach, saying you want to have a better relationship with them and you believe that positive encouragement is the best way.

TIPS FOR GOING FORWARD
1) Make a list of the behaviours you want to discourage in your children (for example, fighting with one another).
2) Make a list of the behaviours you want to encourage (for example, getting along, sharing, playing well together).
3) Write down how you will specifically encourage any signs, however small, of these positive behaviours.

# STEP 5

## USING REWARDS

In the previous sections we looked at how positive parental attention, using encouragement and play, can be influential in promoting good behaviour in young children and in building a close relationship with them. In this section we look at how rewards and treats can be used to encourage children, and to act as back-up to the praise and attention you are providing. Rewards can simply be spontaneous treats given when a child is behaving well. For example, 'Thanks for helping with the cleaning up, now I've time to read you a story – which one would you like?' or 'You worked hard on your homework, well done, would you like an ice-pop from the freezer?' Rewards can also be planned in advance and given for an agreed behaviour. To illustrate this, let's look at how one mother positively solved a problem she was facing with the help of a reward system.

## Using a Star Chart

Jean had a problem with her six-year-old daughter Mary, who just wouldn't go to bed on time. Mary would moan and whine at bedtime and think of excuses to delay the process, saying 'I'm hungry' or 'I need something to drink'. Jean tried many things to get her to go to bed, like cajoling, lecturing, etc., but the more she tried to get her to hurry, the more Mary would dawdle. Even when she got her to her room and into bed, five minutes later, Mary would be up again. Jean was exasperated at this and would often lose her patience with Mary.

Talking to her Public Health Nurse, Jean got the idea to use a star chart with Mary to help her go to bed on time. She sat down with Mary to explain about the chart in advance. She explained why Mary needed to go to bed on time and how she had a new star chart to help her do this. She explained that Mary would get a silver star for being in  bed by 8pm (that meant that Mary had to start getting ready by 7.30pm) and if she stayed in bed she would get a gold star the next morning. When Mary had five stars she would get an extra treat. Jean asked Mary what she would like as a treat and Mary said an ice-cream. The two of them made up the chart together, divided into the different days, with spaces on each day for two stars. Mary coloured in the outside of the chart and Jean stuck a picture of Mary asleep on it, to remind her of what the chart was for. They agreed to hang the chart on the bedside wall, where Dad could also see it in the morning.

On the first night, with a little support, Mary got into bed by

8pm. Jean praised her, and took out a star and Mary pinned it on the chart. Mary settled down, but ten minutes later she left her room. Jean knew how to handle this: she didn't give out to her or give too much attention, but calmly directed Mary back to her room. In the morning, Mary asked about getting a gold star. Jean explained that she would have to stay in her room for the night to get the gold star. That evening, Mary went to bed on time and got her silver star and a kiss from Mum. She asked about the gold star and Jean reminded her about staying in the bedroom all night. Sure enough, Mary did this and she got the gold star in the morning. Jean was so pleased about it that she told Mary's father as well.

As time went on Mary became more used to going to bed on time and staying there until morning. There were still times when she would go to bed late, or come out of her room, but Jean managed these times by firmly insisting that Mary returned to her room, and by ensuring she got little attention when she was out of her room. Jean also made sure not to give the gold star in the morning.

MAKING REWARDS EFFECTIVE
The above example illustrates how a reward system can be used as a back-up to encouragement for a younger child. It highlights a number of principles, which make planned rewards effective:

### Be clear about the behaviour you want
Often when giving rewards parents are vague about what they want, for example, giving a child a treat for 'being good'. Also, parents often reward the absence of a negative behaviour they don't want, for example, 'not fighting' or 'not staying up late'. The trouble with these approaches is that they don't tell the child exactly what you want and in the latter example they highlight

the behaviour you don't want. For this reason it is important to be very clear and positive about the behaviour you do want and to make sure the child is clear as well. In the above example Jean rewarded Mary for being in bed at 8pm and for staying in her room until morning, both very clear and positive behaviours.

### Use motivating rewards

It is important to use rewards which are of great interest to your child, and which they will work hard for. This varies from child to child and depends very much on your child's age. For younger children, brightly-coloured stickers or stars, backed up by small treats, can be enough to motivate them. Older children won't be motivated by stars but will usually be motivated by a points system for good behaviour, leading to tangible rewards for a certain amount of points, such as increased pocket money. Rewards don't have to be expensive to be effective. Even older children can be motivated by ordinary treats like extra playtime, a special trip, etc. It is important to put some time into thinking which rewards will work for your child. It often helps to ask the child what he or she would like (within limits) as Jean did in the above example.

Examples of good rewards are:

- staying up later
- special time with parents in the evening
- an extra bedtime story
- going shopping with a parent
- a trip to McDonalds
- going to the cinema
- having a friend over
- 20 pence extra pocket money

### Involve children in the planning

The more children are 'hooked in' and involved in the planning of rewards, the more likely the rewards are to be effective. As seen in the above example, it is a good idea to explain in advance the reward system and the positive reasons for it, making sure the child understands what you want, and answering any questions he or she has. Equally, getting the child involved in making the chart, choosing the stars, etc., all make a difference to the child's motivation. Notice how Jean let Mary colour in the chart and then let her pin the stars onto it.

OF COURSE ORIGINALLY DAD'S REWARD SYSTEM STARTED SMALL...

### Start small

One of the reasons reward systems can sometimes fail is that they may initially be too difficult for the child, and when the child fails to get the reward on the first few attempts he or she gives up, feeling disillusioned. For this reason it is important to start small, with behaviour that is easy enough for the child to achieve. For example, with a child who finds it hard to concentrate, instead of only rewarding him for doing his homework for a whole hour, you could reward him with a star for every fifteen minutes he spends concentrating. In the above example, Jean made the task easier for Mary by dividing it into two parts – being in bed at 8pm and staying in her room until morning.

### Use lots of encouragement

Rewards aren't a replacement for verbal encouragement and approval. In fact, they work best if they are backed up by lots of positive attention and kind words. Getting others to notice and be involved in reward systems can be very helpful. Notice how Mary's chart was placed on her bedroom wall for her Dad to see and thus add his approval and encouragement.

Rewards work best if they are not used excessively, but only for special occasions or to learn specific behaviours. When a child has learned the desired behaviour the reward system can be phased out over time. For example, when Mary gets into the habit of going to bed on time, Jean can phase out the star system, replacing it with ordinary positive attention. If Mary is still motivated to gain stars, a new desired behaviour can be selected, such as doing her homework at a specified time or coming in when asked.

#### TIPS FOR GOING FORWARD

1) Make a list of the rewards that you know will really motivate your children, and which you can easily afford and are happy to give them.

2) Plan with your children a star chart or points system for a specific new behaviour you want to teach them.

# STEP 6

## SETTING RULES AND HELPING CHILDREN KEEP THEM

### HOW MANY RULES?

Parents rightly feel obliged to teach their children good social behaviour. While it is important to teach children to think for themselves and to be self-responsible, it is also important to set certain rules and limits and to correct them when they step outside these. You may wonder what is the best way to do this. How can we set rules and limits with children in a way that teaches them self-responsibility? In addition, when we have set a rule, what is the best way to ensure children keep them, or learn from the consequences if they don't? These are the questions we will attempt to answer in this section.

Firstly, encourage children to make as many decisions for themselves as possible. Letting them make many decisions and choices helps them to be independent and to grow up confident and responsible. Many parents create unnecessary rules and lose the opportunity to let children decide about different things. For example, does a parent have to decide what colour socks her five-year-old wears? Does a parent have to decide what toys a child chooses in play? Do the grown-ups always have to decide what the family has for dinner? Of course the decisions children can make and those that a parent must make for them depend very much on their age.

Secondly, give children choices even when you are imposing a limit. For example, you may insist a child does her homework when she comes in from school, but you may give her choices about when and where she does it, provided it is done well. Or you may insist a child eats vegetables with his dinner but let him choose (within reason) which vegetables. Or you may insist a child goes to bed at 8pm but give her choices about the routine prior to going to bed. By giving children options within the limits you set, and by negotiating these with them, you increase their co-operation and self-responsibility.

Thirdly, keep the rules you set with children to a minimum, confining them to those that really matter. One of the errors parents can make is to have too many rules for their children. This is especially true when children are demanding and parents wish to take control. However, too many rules often leads to more conflict, which in turn reduces even further the amount of time children co-operate with their parents' wishes. For this reason it is best to keep rules and commands to a minimum, and focus only on the rules that really matter to you. Once these are chosen, it is important to work hard to ensure that your children comply with them.

EFFECTIVE COMMANDS/ASSERTIVE COMMANDS
People often fall into the trap of issuing commands to children either aggressively or passively, rather than assertively. With aggressive commands, we are more likely to use an angry voice and intimidating body language. However, this can be ineffective, only resulting in the child getting angry in return. Even if the child does what we ask, he or she is likely to be hurt or resentful and less likely to comply in the future.

With passive commands we use a soft whispery voice, hardly gaining the child's attention. In this case the child is likely to ignore what we say or not carry out the request because he or she feels we don't really mean it.

With assertive commands we insist on gaining the child's attention, by getting down to his or her level, gaining eye

AND ONE OF THE RULES OF THIS HOUSE IS THAT WE DISCOURAGE AGGRESSION!!

contact, cutting out distractions, etc. We use a calm, polite and firm voice, while keeping our body language friendly but firm.

Assertive commands are not only the most respectful for both parent and child, they are also by far the most effective way to help children co-operate and do what we say. Learning how to communicate assertively takes a lot of practice, as often we are not aware of what our body language is communicating. Sometimes people communicate with a glaring expression on their face or a trembling in their voice but are unaware of this. Role play is one of the best ways to practice, either in a group where you can get feedback from other participants, or at home in front of a mirror where you can observe yourself. (You might want to make sure no one else is in the house at the time!)

## USE POSITIVE COMMANDS

As an experiment, I want you to carry out the following instruction in your imagination. I want you not to think of a blue kangaroo. Don't think of a blue kangaroo!

Were you able to carry out this simple instruction? On average most people find it impossible to carry out a negative command like this because, to understand what is being asked, you have to visualise a blue kangaroo. Giving negative or 'don't' commands to children creates the same problem. If we say 'don't' to a child, for example, 'Don't run in the shop', the child has to visualise himself running in the shop to understand what we mean. Such a command immediately focuses him on the behaviour we don't want and acts almost as a suggestion to carry it out. In addition, 'don't' commands only tell children what they can't do (something they often know very well!), and nothing about what they can do. With 'don't' commands we give few ideas to children about how to behave correctly. Equally, we are more likely to give 'don't' commands angrily, and this sets up the expectation that the child is about to misbehave. For this reason I suggest you issue only positive 'do' commands to children. All negatively framed commands can be made positive. All 'don'ts' can be turned into 'dos'.

For example:
- 'Don't grab the toys from your sister' can become 'Please ask your sister to share the toys'.
- 'Don't shout in the house' can become 'Please use a quiet voice in the house'.
- 'Don't hurt your little brother' can become 'Please look after your little brother'.

### GIVE CHILDREN TIME TO COMPLY

One of the biggest mistakes that parents make is that they don't give children time to comply with a command. They bunch commands together and may have given three or four before the child has had a chance to carry out the first one. This leaves the child confused and burdened and invariably leads to conflict. When you ask a child to do something, I suggest you wait about five seconds before you issue another command or before taking disciplinary action. It can be helpful to count to five silently in your head. This

CLEAN THE KITCHEN!
MOW THE LAWN! TIDY
YOUR ROOM... AND STOP
RUNNING AROUND SO
MUCH!

helps to diffuse the situation, and gives children time to decide how to comply.

Warnings and reminders are also helpful to children. For example, when children are engrossed in play before bedtime it can be helpful to remind them of bedtime by saying, for example, 'You will have to get ready for bed in ten minutes'. This gives children time to prepare and make choices about how to end their play.

### PRAISE CO-OPERATION

It is important to get into the habit of praising children when they co-operate with your wishes. Commenting positively each time they do what you ask takes any 'power victory' out of the experience, and helps children see it as rewarding to be co-operative.

Often parents don't feel like thanking a child when they do something they are told, or they feel it is something the child should do anyway without praise. However, the problem with this approach is that behaviour not rewarded soon disappears. If parents wish to encourage their children's co-operation, thanking them when they do what they are told can make all the difference.

### FOLLOWING THROUGH ON COMMANDS

Even when parents follow all the suggestions above and give their children clear, assertive and positive commands, there will still be times when a child chooses not to comply. It is normal, and indeed healthy, for children to test their parents' rules and limits. Parents must respond to this challenge and ensure children experience the consequences of such testing. This helps them learn to co-operate and understand the effects of their actions.

LOGICAL CONSEQUENCES

We can not make anyone do what they decide not to. This is especially the case with children. All we can do is offer children a choice between doing what we ask and a consequence for not doing so. The goal is to make it rewarding for them to take the choice we suggest and have an unrewarding consequence when they don't. The more logical these consequences are, the more powerful the lesson is. Examples of good logical consequences are as follows:

- If a child doesn't eat at mealtime, then no food is made available until the next mealtime even though the child is hungry – the child learns to eat at mealtimes.
- If a child stays off school (possibly feigning illness), then he or she stays in bed for the day – the child learns it is not fun to stay off school.
- If a child comes in one hour late, then he or she has to be in one hour earlier the next evening – the child learns to come in on time.
- If a child has made a mess, then he or she has to clean it up before going out to play – the child learns not to make a mess.
- If a child gets aggressive during playtime, then playtime ends – the child learns to play appropriately.
- If a child dawdles getting ready for bed, then there is no time for a story – the child learns to get ready for bed quickly.
- If a child does not get up by eight in the morning, then he or she has to go to bed an hour earlier – the child learns to get up on time.

Consequences such as those listed above are best offered to children in the form of choices and, if possible, thought out in advance, as it can be difficult to think of them in the heat of the moment. For example, 'You either play with the sand and keep it in the box, or it will be taken away from you – it's your choice' or, 'You can either calm down now and play the game, or the game will stop – it's your choice'.

When you do set up a consequence in the form of a choice, you must be prepared to enforce it and follow it through. The essential thing about enforcing consequences is that it is a time for action and not words. It is best if a parent follows through calmly and firmly without reasoning or scolding. Things can be talked about at another time. Enforcing consequences is a time for action.

WHEN–THEN COMMAND

A simple command which gets great results for parents is the when-then command. This is a positive command which orders events so that children experience a natural reward following the completion of a task or chore. For example, you can say 'Paul, when you do your homework, then you can watch TV'. Paul is given the choice of doing his homework and then having the reward of watching TV, or the choice of not doing his homework and having the consequence of not watching TV. Other examples are:

YOU CAN WATCH
TV AS SOON AS YOU
TIDY YOUR ROOM...
BECAUSE BY THEN
WE MAY HAVE
FOUND THE TV!

'When you do your homework, then you can go out to play.'
'When you get ready for bed, then Mummy will read you a story.'

The command can also be rephrased using the words as soon as. For example:
'You can have some desert as soon as you finish your dinner.'
'You can watch TV as soon as you get dressed.'

A FORMULA TO HELP CHILDREN COMPLY WITH COMMANDS
The following step-by-step sequence gives you a formula for issuing effective commands to children and then helping them to comply by following through with logical consequences:

1) Give the child a clear, positive and assertive command (for example, 'Paul, please turn off the TV now and do your homework').
2) Wait about five seconds for the child to comply.
3) If the child complies, praise him ('Thank you for doing that, Paul').
4) If the child does not comply, give him the choice of a consequence (for example, 'Paul, you can either turn off the TV yourself or I will, which do you prefer?').
5) If child complies, praise him.
6) If not, enforce consequence (parent goes and turns off the TV).
7) Be sure to ignore protests.

TIPS FOR GOING FORWARD
1) Make a list of decisions that your children can be encouraged to make for themselves (for example, what games to play, the order of homework subjects).

2) Make a list of the rules that are important for your children to keep (for example, no hitting out, 8pm bedtime).
3) Pick one or two rules which you want to work on next week. Write them down in the form of clear, polite, assertive requests (for example, 'John, please put away your toys', 'Mary, when you finish your homework you can go outside').
4) Pick a logical consequence to each of these requests, should your child choose not to comply. You may be able to think of more than one.
5) Follow the step-by-step formula to help enforce the requests you make.

## STEP 7

### IGNORING MISBEHAVIOUR

In the first four steps we showed how important parents' attention is to their children. We talked about how you can provide your child with lots of positive approving attention, through play, encouragement and rewards.

In Step 7 we look at the opposite technique – stopping negative behaviour by reducing the attention it receives. We need to remember that even negative attention such as giving out, criticising or shouting all give some attention to the misbehaviour and make it likely to continue. Behaviours such as tantrums, whingeing and minor squabbles depend on the attention of an audience and can be eliminated if they are actively ignored.

### WHAT IS IGNORING?

Ignoring misbehaviour is about paying it as little attention as possible. It is about not getting drawn into rows or screaming matches, but instead remaining calm and not taking the 'bait' of

YOU KNOW, SO FAR IGNORING MISBEHAVIOUR HASN'T BEEN AS HARD AS I THOUGHT...

children's misbehaviour. It could be sitting out a young child's tantrum, not responding to a child's nagging, or calmly walking away from an older child's protests. It is also about not taking misbehaviour personally and not dwelling on it. While a child's misbehaviour can be very upsetting, good ignoring is about not letting it get to you, or not holding on to it, but moving on from it quickly to find examples of good behaviour you want.

Ignoring is definitely not easy. In fact it may be the hardest idea introduced in this booklet. Many parents think they are ignoring a behaviour but are inadvertently giving it attention via their body language, for example by looking stern or disapproving, or by the fact that they are getting annoyed or emotional. While the child is receiving this type of unconscious attention the behaviour will still continue. Equally, the silent treatment or not talking to someone for the day is not active ignoring. Indeed, such strategies can be counter-productive, building up resentment in both parent and child.

### Ignoring Is Not an Alternative to Positive Approving Attention

Ignoring is only effective when there are other times during which children receive warm approving attention from their parents. For this reason I emphasise the first four steps in this booklet, which are about providing positive attention to children and forming good and enjoyable relationships with them. These positive experiences are like investments in the 'bank', to be used at times of conflict or misbehaviour. When children see their parents' attention as valuable or when there are many positive times between parents and children, they are more likely to work to seek parental approval. Children are more likely to give up negative behaviours when parental attention is withdrawn.

## Target specific behaviours

Active ignoring works best if it is used to target specific behaviours. Parents should plan in advance which behaviours they want to reduce and whether they can ignore these. Remember, it is up to parents to decide which behaviours they can ignore and this can vary from family to family. For example, some parents can ignore their children's swearing, but others feel this needs to be dealt with by another sanction (for example, 'Time Out' – see Step 8). The types of behaviours with which ignoring can work very effectively are:

- whingeing
- temper tantrums
- smart talk
- cheek
- protests
- messy eating
- pulling faces
- minor squabbles
- swearing

## Ignore thoroughly

Active ignoring involves giving no attention whatsoever to the child's behaviour. This means turning the body completely away and making no eye contact. It is also important to have a calm, relaxed expression on your face. If you communicate that you are angry or upset through your body language, the child may feel that he has 'got to you' and that you are likely to give in if he persists.

### Ignore consistently

Active ignoring is not easy, especially when it is first applied. Children may have learned that the best way to get their parents to do what they want is by whingeing and kicking up a fuss. When the parent responds differently by not giving in, the child may intensify the whingeing and shouting to get them to change their mind, before giving up and trying something else. In a nutshell, the behaviour may get worse before it gets better. If you decide to use active ignoring as a tactic you must be prepared to apply it consistently each time the target behaviour occurs and to follow it through on each occasion.

#### RETURN POSITIVE ATTENTION AS SOON AS POSSIBLE

When a child does give up the negative behaviour, for example, when she gives up protesting or the tantrum stops, it is important to return positive attention, perhaps with a distraction or the suggestion of some positive activity. This is often not easy as the parent may be angry and upset after a period of misbehaviour and may use the opportunity now that the child is 'quiet' to scold or give out to her. However, this can restart the misbehaviour and stop the child learning the value of good positive behaviour.

Active ignoring only really works when it is completed with a return to positive attention. As you become more thorough in your ignoring, the period of misbehaviour will become quite short as the child learns that nothing can be gained by persisting and begins to change her behaviour to seek the benefits of your positive attention.

### Continue to encourage positive behaviour

If you do decide to ignore a certain behaviour, you can double the impact of this by targeting the opposite positive behaviour with specific encouragement. For example, if you are going to ignore minor squabbles when they occur between your children, it is important to praise them any time you see them getting along better, or sharing with each other.

With younger children it can be helpful to give them distractions and specific suggestions of other positive behaviours instead of the misbehaviour. For example: 'No, you may not turn on the television, but you may play with your Lego' or 'Why don't you do some drawing instead?'

## REMAIN CALM

Perhaps the most difficult aspect of effective ignoring is remaining calm. It is no surprise that stress management or relaxation techniques are among the biggest selling topics in books within the health field. In most book shops you will find hundreds of books which detail excellent ideas on remaining calm and controlling stress. Below are some of the main ways people remain calm in difficult situations and I suggest you seek further information as you need it.

### Think differently

When people are angry or upset they are usually thinking in a negative way about the situation they are in. For example, when confronted by your child's misbehaviour you might think 'He's doing this on purpose'

RIGHT! IF YOU DON'T TELL ME WHICH OF YOU MESSED UP MY RELAXATION TAPE, I'M GOING TO GO BERSERK!!

or 'This will never change'. Such thoughts are likely to make you more angry and helpless. However, if you can think differently during these situations this can really help you cope better. Imagine if, instead of thinking the above, you say to yourself, 'This is a bad day for her, she's probably tired, she'll be better tomorrow' or 'She's testing the limits today, the best way for me to help her change is to firmly and calmly respond'. Such positive thoughts will have the effect of making you feel calmer and more capable of dealing with the situation.

### Talk things through

Talking through how you feel with a partner or friend away from the conflict can be very helpful. Telling someone how negative you feel at times can make these feelings more manageable and less overwhelming. In this way it is very important to create supportive relationships in your life, where you can 'let off steam' if you need to.

### Practice relaxation

Learning to relax is something which gets easier with practice. When people take time out each day to relax they can more easily draw on this resource in conflict. There are many different ways to relax such as:

- Deep breathing exercises or meditation
- Muscular relaxation or special exercises (for example, yoga)
- Positive visualisation (for example, recalling in your mind beautiful and relaxing scenes, from a holiday perhaps, or a favourite lake walk)
- Doing something you really enjoy such as reading, walking or even doing the garden

The trick with relaxation is to make it a daily habit. The more you know what it feels like to be relaxed and the more you practice being relaxed, the more easily you will be able to switch into that mode in a stressful situation. Remember, you feel nearly as relaxed recalling a peaceful time as you did during that peaceful time!

TIPS FOR GOING FORWARD

1) Target one or two behaviours which you can actively ignore next week to eliminate them (for example, whingeing and protesting).

2) Identify the positive opposite behaviours and plan to encourage, praise and reward them each time they occur (when your child does what they are asked quietly and without protest).

3) Take time out to relax next week.

4) Visualise yourself calmly responding to a discipline problem, and not giving attention to the misbehaviour.

## TIME OUT AND OTHER SANCTIONS

For difficult behaviours which cannot be ignored, and for children who consistently do not do what their parents tell them, a technique called Time Out can be very useful in helping parents manage. Time Out is basically a way of interrupting difficult behaviour, and breaking from an interaction that is negative and damaging. It teaches children how to separate from a situation and how to calm down. It gives parents a means of discipline which allows them to feel in control, which respects the child and which is a much more realistic, effective and acceptable alternative than slapping.

Time Out is a formalised version of what parents have being doing for years when confronted with their children's misbehaviour – sending them to their room to calm down or asking them to stand in the corner or outside the door. In this section I suggest a formula for Time Out which can make it effective in most circumstances.

YES IT'S BETTER IF YOU CHOOSE TO GO TO 'TIME OUT' YOURSELF... AND NO YOU CAN'T CHOOSE IT WHEN IT'S TIME TO VISIT YOUR GRANNY.

## EXPLAIN TIME OUT IN ADVANCE

It is important to sit down with children in advance to explain to them about Time Out. It is important to be positive about the purpose, for example, you might explain that it is about helping them to get on better together, or learning better ways of resolving disagreements other than hitting out. Explain that it is about helping everyone – children and parents – to calm down in angry situations, and avoid rows and shouting which might otherwise occur. There are a number of key points that need to be covered in the explanation:

### Which behaviour?

Children need to be absolutely clear which behaviour will lead to Time Out (for example, hitting out, or breaking things). Parents should stick to this and not include other behaviours in the heat of the moment.

### Where?

Children should know where Time Out will take place. This ideally should be a safe place where there are not too many distractions. A hallway or bedroom is often used. For younger children, a chair facing the corner can be sufficient, though it may be necessary to have a back-up room if the child refuses to stay in the chair. The Time Out place should not be a scary or unsafe place such as a shed or a bathroom where medicines are kept. If you feel the child is likely to be distressed by going to Time Out you may wish to show him exactly where he will have to go in advance, reassuring him that it is simply a way of helping him to behave better.

## How long?

Research shows that Time Out only needs to be short (about five minutes) to be effective. It should not be longer than ten minutes unless the child continues to make a fuss. The essential rule is that children need to be quiet for at least two minutes before they can come out. This means that if they protest, shout or scream, they will have to stay there longer. The goal of Time Out is to interrupt negative behaviour and to help children learn self-control and how to calm down. If they are let out while they are protesting or still angry, this defeats the purpose.

### A FORMULA FOR IMPLEMENTING TIME OUT

1) Misbehaviour occurs.
2) Parent gives warning if appropriate – 'If you throw another toy you will have to go to Time Out'. (For some behaviours, for example, hitting, a warning may not be appropriate and the child should immediately go to Time Out.)
3) Misbehaviour occurs again, so parent insists child goes to Time Out.
4a) For a child under five. If the child refuses, he can be guided by the hand to the Time Out chair. The parent should do this calmly and firmly, avoiding getting drawn into an argument.
5a) If the child does not stay in a Time Out chair, he can be placed in a back-up place (such as the hallway).
4b) For a child over five. If the child refuses, the parent adds on extra minutes to Time Out up to a maximum of ten minutes (for example, 'That is six minutes for arguing').
5b) If the child continues to refuse, the parent offers a choice between Time Out and a back-up sanction – 'You either choose to go to Time Out for ten minutes or you miss X (favourite TV programme)… it's your choice'.

6b) If the child refuses, the back-up sanction is enforced and Time Out is dropped.

### A Formula for Ending Time Out

1) The parent ensures the child stays in Time Out for the selected period or until the child has been quiet for at least two minutes. It is important that the parent does not give in to the child's protests or screams, otherwise he will learn that the way to get out of Time Out is by protesting.
2) If the child refuses to come out of Time Out at the end of the time period, the parent simply ignores this and makes no comment.
3) When the child comes out of Time Out the parent does not criticise or nag about the misbehaviour, but is pleasant, offering the child a suggestion of new positive behaviour (for example, 'Do you want to go and play now?'). The misbehaviour has now been dealt with.

### Using Back-up Sanctions To Make Time Out Effective

Time Out is essentially about giving a child a choice. The crucial thing is to help the child choose voluntarily to go there. This helps the child learn self-control and take responsibility. If a child refuses to go to Time Out, having a back-up sanction can be very effective. For example, the parent can offer the child a choice, 'You either choose to go to Time Out or you miss your favourite TV programme.' It is crucial that parents think ahead about the type of

sanctions they might use, so that in any discipline situation they will have a range of options open to them. Sanctions are best if:

### They are short

Research shows that sanctions can work just as well if they are short. Being grounded for one afternoon can be enough to ensure the child has learned his lesson. If sanctions go on too long, for example being grounded for a month, they can become unenforceable and cause resentment in the child. Another advantage of short sanctions is that the child can get back on track and have new opportunities to behave well as soon as possible.

### They affect mainly the child

It is pointless for parents to choose a sanction which penalises themselves as much or even more than the child, for example when a parent has to miss the football match he also wanted to go to! It is best to choose a sanction which involves the child and not the parent experiencing the loss.

### They are within the control of the parent

It is best if the parent can easily enforce the sanction. For example, ensuring the child does extra chores may be difficult for some families and it may be better to opt for something else, such as loss of pocket money. The choice of sanctions is individual to each family and child.

### They are logically related to the misbehaviour

For example, if a child has hit a friend, it is logical that the child is not allowed to visit that friend for tea. Other examples of possible sanctions are:

- Not being allowed to watch TV for one evening.

- Not being allowed use the bike for one afternoon
- Being grounded for a day
- Missing a favourite TV programme
- No playtime
- Cancelling a trip
- Losing pocket money
- Earlier bedtime
- Not being able to choose a video.

### TIME OUT FOR PARENTS

Time Out is essentially about interrupting an escalating row or a negative way of communicating. Often in discipline situations parents can get so frustrated that they lose their own tempers or become very upset. At these times it is likely that you will say or do something you regret. It is important for parents to find ways of stopping this escalating – nipping this anger 'in the bud'. Time Out used for parents themselves is a good way of achieving this – when you feel yourself getting too angry or upset to deal with a situation you can choose to withdraw from the child in order to calm down. You can then return to the situation when you are in a better frame of mind.

### TIPS FOR GOING FORWARD

1) Identify a behaviour for which you could use Time Out. Plan it carefully, deciding when, where and how.

2) Make a list of sanctions which you can use as back-up for Time Out.

3) Follow the step-by-step formula as a way of making Time Out effective.

4) Use Time Out for yourself if you feel you are becoming too angry in a discipline situation.

# STEP 9

## TALKING THINGS THROUGH

The most effective long-term way to help children behave well is to talk problems through with them. This helps children to understand their own feelings and those of other people, to think through the consequences of their actions and to discover positive alternatives to misbehaviour which are good for them and other people.

Often parents make the mistake of trying to talk a problem through with a child at the time of conflict. As discussed in previous sections, what is called for at these times is withdrawing attention from the misbehaviour and helping children learn by experiencing consequences to their actions.

It is better to talk problems through with children away from the conflict situation at a different time when everyone has calmed down. It is a good idea to set up a particular time where you can sit down with the child when you both won't be distracted and which doesn't conflict with anything else (don't select a time during your child's favourite TV programme). In addition, try and allow a bit of time for problem-solving sessions, as talking things through with children can take time. Rushing can prevent either parent or child from being heard and may lead to conflict.

Talking things through can be divided into four separate stages: Listening, Speaking Up, Generating Solutions, Planning / Agreements. These four stages involve good communication skills and are the basis of most problem-solving methods (including those used in business and even international peace negotiations!).

## 1) ACTIVE LISTENING

Listening is probably the most important communication skill of all. When we truly listen, we step out of our own shoes into those of another person. We try to understand the world as they see it, not just as we see it. Such listening is a great service to another person as we all need to be understood. Being understood by another person helps us to understand ourselves. Active listening is very important to children. As well as being the best form of positive attention, it helps them understand their thoughts and feelings and those of other people, as well as bringing parent and child closer together.

Yet listening is also probably the most difficult skill of all. Most of us have no training in it and it requires a lot of effort on the part of the listener, especially when there is conflict between the listener and the person being listened to. Children in particular are often not listened to. Their thoughts, feelings and viewpoints generally aren't seen as being as important as those of adults. Instead of listening, parents often fall into the trap of giving advice, criticising, or coaching – all useful skills at times but not when we are actively listening to understand a child's feelings. Consider the following responses to a child:

Paul (upset):  James grabbed the computer game from me.
Parent:        Well, you shouldn't have being playing with it so
               long (criticism); or
               Why don't you play with something else?
               (advice); or
               Oh, don't worry, it's not so bad (coaching); or
               Let me go and talk to James (rescuing).

Active listening involves giving children your full attention. It involves setting aside anything else you are doing to really concentrate on what they are saying (verbally and non-verbally). Perhaps the two most important aspects of listening are: a) reflecting back to children what they are saying so they feel understood and b) acknowledging their feelings. Consider now some alternative listening responses:

Paul (upset):  James grabbed the computer game from me.
Parent:        Sounds like you are upset. Sit down and tell me what happened (sensing the child's feelings and encouraging the child to say more);
               Poor you, I know how much you like playing that game (acknowledging the child's feelings).

In the above examples, the parent is validating the child's feelings and attempting to see the problem from his point of view. Sometimes simply repeating what the child has said, or nodding encouragingly can be sufficient to help the child feel listened to and encouraged to express more.

## 2) SPEAKING UP

After first listening to the child's feelings and point of view, you are now in a position to express your own feelings and viewpoint. Often people get the order of this the wrong way round; they attempt to get their point of view across before listening to the other person. This can lead to a lot of conflict. Skilled communicators and leaders always listen first. When we understand another person's point of view and have acknowledged their feelings, they are far more likely to then be open to listen to us. Expressing your views and concerns also requires skill and tact. Often people fall into the trap of blaming, or not acknowledging their own feelings. Good communicators acknowledge their feelings, express their positive intentions, and focus on what they want. Consider the following examples of ineffective versus effective Speaking Up:

Ineffective: What the hell do you think you are playing at staying out so late? You've really upset me.

Effective: I worry about you going out late at night especially when it's dark. You see, I want you to be safe (expresses feelings as a positive concern using an 'I' message).

Ineffective : You are such an inconsiderate child, you always make me late (excessive blaming, damaging 'you' message).

Effective : I feel frustrated when you don't get up on time for school. You see, it makes me late for work and I need to get to work on time. I would like it to go a lot smoother in the mornings (clear 'I' message, parent focuses on what he or she wants from the child).

### 3) GENERATING SOLUTIONS

Once you have understood your child's point of view and expressed your own feelings, you are now in a position to think with your child of alternative solutions to the problems you are both facing. Rather than simply giving your own solutions it is important to hold back and encourage the child to come up with solutions himself. This can be done by asking questions such as: 'How do you think you can solve this?', 'How can you ensure you get home on time?', 'What other ways can you get a go on the computer without hitting out?' Though it may be tempting to

SO WHAT I'M SAYING IS I'D LIKE YOU TO BE QUIET WHEN I'M WATCHING THE TV NEWS. NOW FOR THE MAIN POINTS OF MY ARGUMENT AGAIN...

come up with your own answers, it is crucial to proceed at the child's pace and to wait for him to generate the solutions. Children are far more likely to carry through solutions they have generated themselves. You will be surprised at how even young children, when given time, can come up with solutions which are as good as or even better than those thought up by parents.

It is important to help children generate as many alternative solutions as possible. Try not to be critical at this stage; encourage your child's creativity and listen to all the ideas he comes up with. These can include solutions tried successfully in the past. For example, you son may remember that when he stayed away from certain boys in the class on previous occasions he didn't get into trouble. Once talked about and understood, these past solutions are more easily repeated.

### 4) PLAN

Now it is time to help the child decide whic solutions he is going to use. During this stage the emphasis is on helping children think through the consequences of the ideas suggested in stage 2, in order to identify those which have the best results, both for them and for other people. Frequently, children come up with unrealistic or inappropriate solutions. However, rather than criticising, you can guide them by asking them to think of the consequences. For example, as a way of getting to use his brother's computer, a child might suggest taking a turn without asking. But on thinking it through he realises that this could get him into more trouble if his brother finds out and refuses to let him use the computer at all.

When the best solution(s) is chosen, it is important to arrange a time to talk again to review how the child is getting on.

To give an example of these four stages in action, consider the following scene, of a father sitting down to talk to his son, who hti another boy at school.

### 1) *Active Listening*

| | |
|---|---|
| Father: | You know I said earlier I wanted to talk to you about what happened in school. |
| John: | It wasn't my fault, Robert started it (whining defensively). |
| Father (calmly): | What happened exactly? (father does not get into a quarrel but listens to the child to hear his perspective). |
| John: | Well, we were out in the yard, playing football. Robert started teasing me so I hit him. |
| Father: | It wasn't very nice of him to call you names. |
| John: | No. |
| Father: | You must have been angry (father picks up on his son's feelings and helps him feel understood). |
| John: | Yes (nods), and then I got into trouble... Mrs O'Reilly sent me to the line. |

| Father: | Sounds like you feel it was unfair, that you think Robert should have got into trouble as well (acknowledges feelings). |
|---|---|
| John: | Yeah. |

## 2) *Speaking Up*

| Father: | Do you know why Mrs O'Reilly sent you to the line? (father helps child think through the consequences of his actions). |
|---|---|
| John: | Because I hit him? |
| Father: | Yeah, while I'm sorry you were called names in school, we have to find other ways of solving it than hitting out. I don't like when you get into trouble in school, because I want you to get on well and be happy there (father expresses his feelings for his son, his positive intentions and what he wants to happen). |

## 3) *Generating Solutions*

| Father: | Can you think of a way to handle it without hitting him? |
|---|---|
| John (thinks): | I don't know. |
| Father: | Come on, you're often very good at school, I am sure you can think of something (father points out that there are times his son behaves well in school, thus encouraging him to think of solutions). |
| John (thinking): | I suppose I could tell him to stop. |
| Father: | Exactly... a perfect way... can you think of anything else? |
| John: | I could just walk away. |
| Father: | You could just walk away... anything else? (father |

|  |  |
|---|---|
| | is encouraging and positive about each of the solutions his child generates. He doesn't put them down or criticise). |
| John: | I could tell the teacher... but she never really listens to me. |
| Father: | I could have a word with her then? |
| John (thinks): | I don't know. |
| Father: | You're not sure about that. Maybe you want to think about that one (father lets child decide, thereby helping him to take responsibility). |
| John | Yeah. |

### 4) *Plan/Agreement*

|  |  |
|---|---|
| Father: | Let's look at what you've got. If Robert jeers at you again, you can just walk away or you can tell him to stop... or you can have a word with your teacher or I could step in and have a word with her... how does that sound? (father summarises the solutions and helps child make a plan). |
| John: | Okay (nods and looks happier). |
| Father: | We will talk again tomorrow to see how you get on; (father sets a time to review the plan). |
| John: | OK, Dad. |

TIPS FOR GOING FORWARD

1) Set aside a time to really listen to your children. This does not only have to be about problems. Listening to your children about the good things in their lives can benefit both parent and child.

2) Rather than always giving solutions to your children's problems, make an effort to hold back and to help them generate their own solutions.

FURTHER READING

Dinkmeyer, D. and D. G. McKay, *STEP: Systematic Training for Effective Parenting* (Random House, 1982).

Forehand, R. and N. Long, *Parenting the Strong-willed Child* (Chicago: Contemporary Books, 1996).

Gottman, J., *The Heart of Parenting* (London: Bloomsbury, 1997).

Gordon, T., PET: *Parent Effectiveness Training* (New York: Penguin, 1975).

Green, C., *Toddler Taming* (London: Vermillion, 1992).

Quinn, M. and T. Quinn, *What Can a Parent Do? The Five to Fifteen Basic Parenting Programme* (Belfast: Family Caring Trust, 1995).

Webster-Stratton, C., *The Incredible Years: A Trouble Shooting Guide for Parents of Children Aged 3-8* (Ontario: Umbrella Press, 1992).

FOR GROUP LEADERS
Sharry, J. and Fitzpatrick, C., *Parents Plus Programme: A practical and positive video-based guide to managing and solving discipline problems in children aged 4-11.* (Parents Plus, c/o Mater Child Guidance Clinic, Mater Hospital, North Circular Road, Dublin 7, Tel. 01-853 2426, email: parentsplus@tinet.ie)